The rubbish monster

Written and illustrated by
Braam Jordaan

CAMBRIDGE
UNIVERSITY PRESS

Simphiwe lives in a big house.
Across the road is Hilda's fruit stall.

It is early in the morning.
Simphiwe's front door
opens and he steps outside.
He yawns and stretches.

Then he feels inside his pocket.

"*Sakubona,* Simphiwe!" Mama Hilda
waves. She sees what is in Simphiwe's hand.
"Yo! It is too early to eat chocolate, Simphiwe."

Simphiwe shakes the box. "There is no
chocolate for me. It's empty, Mama."
He throws the box into the street.

"*Aikona*, Simphiwe! Don't litter!"

The chocolate box falls near some empty cans, plastic bags and other rubbish. Suddenly they all begin to shake ...

All the empty cans and bottles, plastic bags
and rubbish roll together into a big heap.

What is it? What is happening?
Is it forming into something?

It has become a monster. A rubbish monster.
   "I'M HUNGRY! FEED ME MORE RUBBISH!"
the rubbish monster roars. Simphiwe runs back
inside his house and slams the door shut.

He peeps out of the window. Oh, no,
the rubbish monster is coming closer
and closer!

Brave Simphiwe opens the front door a
crack. He has found an empty bottle inside.
He throws it at the rubbish monster.

The rubbish monster ducks.

The bottle smashes on the ground.

But look, the pieces of glass are lifting off
the ground.

They are landing on the rubbish monster.

The rubbish monster
is getting bigger and
bigger!

Simphiwe screams,
"Help, Mama. Help!"

Mama Hilda does not know what to do.
Then she sees her friend pushing a trolley
down the street.

"Lucky, look! Please help!" she shouts.

Lucky works for the recycling factory.

"Yes, I can help. Do you have any old newspapers and boxes?"

"Yes! I have old newspapers and fruit boxes for recycling."

"NO, NO! I HATE RECYCLING!"

And as the rubbish monster screams, he grows smaller.

Simphiwe now understands. He has a bright idea. He picks up some of the rubbish and throws it into a dustbin.

"NO, NO! I HATE RUBBISH BINS!" the
rubbish monster screams. He gets smaller
and smaller, weaker and weaker.

Simphiwe, Hilda and Lucky pick up all
the rubbish they can find and put it into
a rubbish bin.

The rubbish monster runs away.

Do you think he will come back?